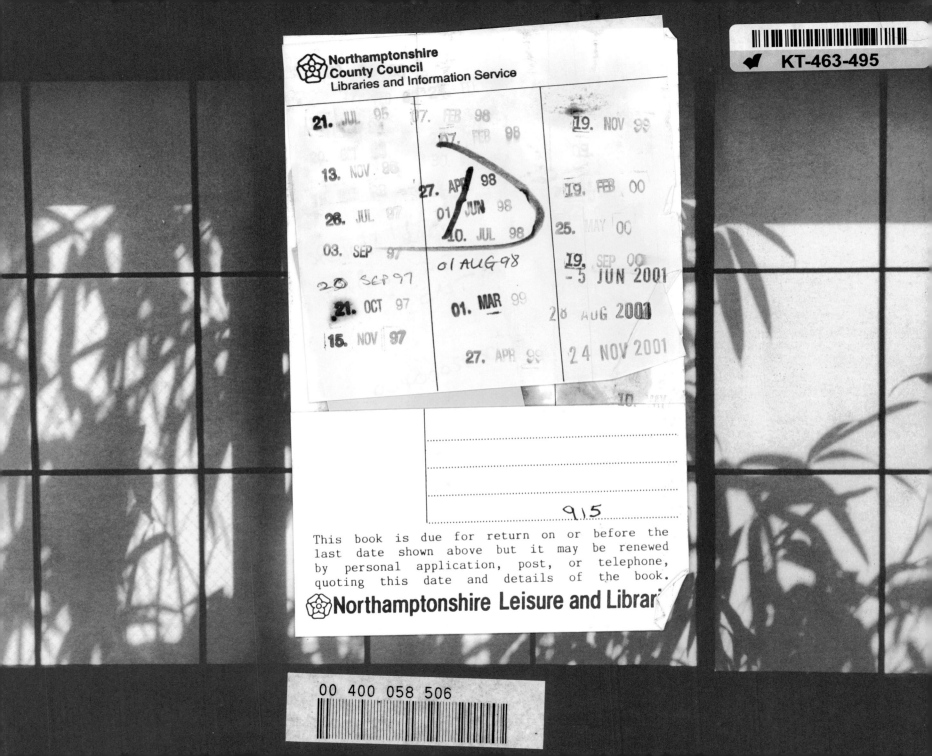

JAPAN
& THE EAST

EARL
SPENCER

To Raine

ISBN 0 9511652 0 8
Published by Earl and Countess Spencer, Althorp,
Northampton NN7 4HG.

Printed in Great Britain by Jolly & Barber Ltd and
bound by Norton Bridge Bookbinders Ltd

FOREWORD

When I was six Father Christmas brought me a box Brownie. It was his last present. After that I moved into the chill world of the grown-ups. But like Alice, I could escape. In my case it was into the Park at Althorp, where bright-eyed squirrels, my pony, foxes, pheasants and geese were recorded by my little camera. In the evening I would lie in wait for herons as they flew to the lake and swooped down to capture the unwary fish.

In Japan, I was reminded of them by the white cranes, on screens, cloisonné and kimonos, symbols of luck and longevity. Nowadays I prefer to photograph people or architecture. On our trip we found enchanting Japanese children, who had seemingly stepped out of a tableau representing their Festival of the Dolls; Chinese traders in Hong Kong; brides in Singapore; an elephant boy in Agra; dancers in Thailand; and in Nepal, a fascinating galaxy of Gurkhas, pedlars, sherpas and holy men. We will always remember the kindness and courtesy shown to us everywhere in Japan, the concern over details, evident also in the meticulous arrangement of their gardens.

On a different scale, Lutyens' concept of New Delhi, for sheer grandeur and imagination, is one of the great sights of the East. Singapore with its go-downs, lush greenery and stunning modern hotels is a remarkable contrast to the serenity of the Himalayan hill country. In Bangkok the houseboats on the klongs, or the tiny houses on stilts, open on the river side to any casual passer-by, all had television. In almost every place we visited, concrete is eroding the traditional houses and Western habits the traditional way of life. In Dubai, the wheel had turned another circle. The spotless streets, the fountains, the swimming pools, the elegant Government buildings, had been successfully imposed upon the desert. Trees grow in the sand, and grass, flowers and shrubs blossom on erstwhile barren soil.

The trip was unforgettable, exciting, interesting, sometimes sad, often funny. I have tried to capture some of my impressions in this personal album. It does not attempt to portray a whole country or a civilisation. I aim to catch a mood, an expression, a building, an occasion, a joke. I offer a glimpse, with affection, into other people's lives.

John Spencer

CONTENTS

93. Houseboats.
94. Washing-up.
95a. Terrace of the Oriental Hotel.
95b. Tropical garden.
96. Thai dancing.
97. Thai boxing.
98. White marble fountain.
99. Geese.
100. Snake and crocodile farm.
101. Poison from the fangs of the python.
102. Florist.
103. Life on the ocean wave.
104. Come dancing.
105. Thai warriors.
106. Barbeque at the Oriental.
107. The local Cash and Carry.
108. Outside the Temple of the Emerald Buddha.
109. Noel Coward suite at the Oriental.
110a. Wats at Bangkok.
110b. Author and his wife.

DELHI & AGRA

111. Arch of Government Building, Delhi.
112. Transport in Agra.
113a. Monkey on a string.
113b. Lahore Gate of the Red Fort.
114. Bougainvillea.
115. The water bearer.
116. Hindu temple.
117a. Snake charmer.
117b. India Gate.
118. Elephant boy.
119. Breakfast-time.
120. Snake Charmer.
121. The Courts of Justice, Delhi.
122. Himalayan bear.
123. Pavilion at Agra.
124. Cobra.
125. View of plain in Hindustan.
126. Palace at Fatehpur Sikri.
127. "A policeman's lot is not a happy one".
128. Onlookers.

129. Lutyens building, New Delhi.
130. Animal trainer.
131. South Block, New Delhi.
132. Gardens of the Taj Mahal.
133. Side view of the Taj Mahal.
134a. Renovations.
134b. Pavilion of the Taj Mahal.
135. Fatehpur Sikri.
136a. Pavilion of the Taj Mahal.
136b. Sari in a breeze.

NEPAL

137. Temple at Bhaktapur.
138. Welcome to Nepal.
139. Foothills of the Himalayas.
140. Hill country.
141. Gurkha children.
142. Timber cutting.
143. Mountain pass.
144. The helicopter pad.
145. Rehearsal for the King's Birthday Parade.
146. Nepalese Palace.
147. The Cavalry.
148. Market in Kathmandu.
149. Spectator with umbrella.
150. Palace for diplomatic receptions.
151a. Sentry guarding holy shrine.
151b. Buddha shielded from ugly sights.
152. Bearded man.
153. Durbar Square, Bhaktapur.
154. Guardians of Nyatapola Temple.
155. Children in Bhaktapur.
156a. Old lady.
157b. Pedlar with his wares.
158. Gurkha military band.
159. Everest Tours.
160. Views from the balcony.
161a. Mother and baby.
161b. The bargain hunter.
162. Fox pelts for sale.
163a. Nepalese architecture.
163b. The universal drink.

164. Gurkha warriors.
165a. The eyes of Buddha.
165b. The eyes of a neighbour.
166. One of the family.
167. Street in Kathmandu.
168. The school bus — 4.00 pm, the world over.
169. The best view.
170. The flute player.
171. The vegetable carriers
172. The end of the journey.
173. Dreaming of a party?
174. Holy men.
175. The woolly hat.
176. A side street in Bhaktapur.
177. Nepalese women.
178. Open-air market in Kathmandu.
179. Having a good scratch.
180. Reading.
181. East and West.
182. "All that glisters is not gold."
183. Friends.
184. Enjoying the joke.
185. Nepalese paintings.
186. In the square.
187. Fortune telling.
188. The vegetable market.

DUBAI & SHARJAH

189. Silhouettes in the new Souk, Sharjah.
190. Shipping in the Creek, Dubai.
191. Grass and shrubs in the desert.
192. The Municipality, Dubai.
193. Entrance to the Palace of H.H Sheik Al Maktoum.
194. Palace by the sea.
195. The Souk at Sharjah.
196. The fish market, Sharjah.
197a. What a big one!
197b. The buyer.
198. View of the Souk.
199. The fruit market.
200. Friendly shopkeeper.

KYOTO

TOKYO

タクシー乗
TAXI
STATION

スペンサー家とワイン

スペンサー家は英国でも由緒ある家柄でジョン·スペンサー卿の頃, 1508年からオルソープに庭園と堀のあるエリザベス王朝様式の大邸宅を構えました. 以来現在に至るまで邸宅は幾代にも受けつがれ, 各時代においてスペンサー家の人々には, 国王の使節として又州知事, 国務大臣松密院長官侍従長, 閣内相, 財務長官, トラファルガー海戦の海軍大臣大蔵大臣等を歴任し, 又, 英国農業界にも大きく貢献致しました. このスペンサー家が特に選りすぐったワインとシャンペンがオルソープの名で英国で販売されております.

THE ORIGIN OF THE MONUMENT OF POEMS
CONPOSED ON SCENIC BEAUTY OF KAMEOKA

This park was under the management of the feudal lord
of Satsuma, Shigehide Shimazu. In 1804, he selected ten
fine scenes in the park on which 9 lords and Hayashi-
Daigakunokami, famous Confucianist and advisor to the
Shogunate, composed in praise of the garden respectively.
The monument has poems in memory of the occasion.
After the Restoration of Meiji, the park belonged to
Count Munenori Terajima, State Councilor. In 1880,
the Emperor Meiji was pleased to visit this site and
enjoyed a Noh performance.

この林園は寛文九年薩摩の島津家が

幕府から壹萬坪の地を下付されたのを、

二十六代藩主重豪のとき隠居して別邸

を営み、苑内の形勝を選んで亀岡十勝

と称し記念の詩碑を建てた。詩の作者は

紀州大納言以下九名の文人諸侯および

林大学頭で、時に文化元年であった。

維新の後、参議寺島宗則の有となり

明治十三年六月九日、明治天皇が行幸

して観能されたので、聖蹟に指定された。

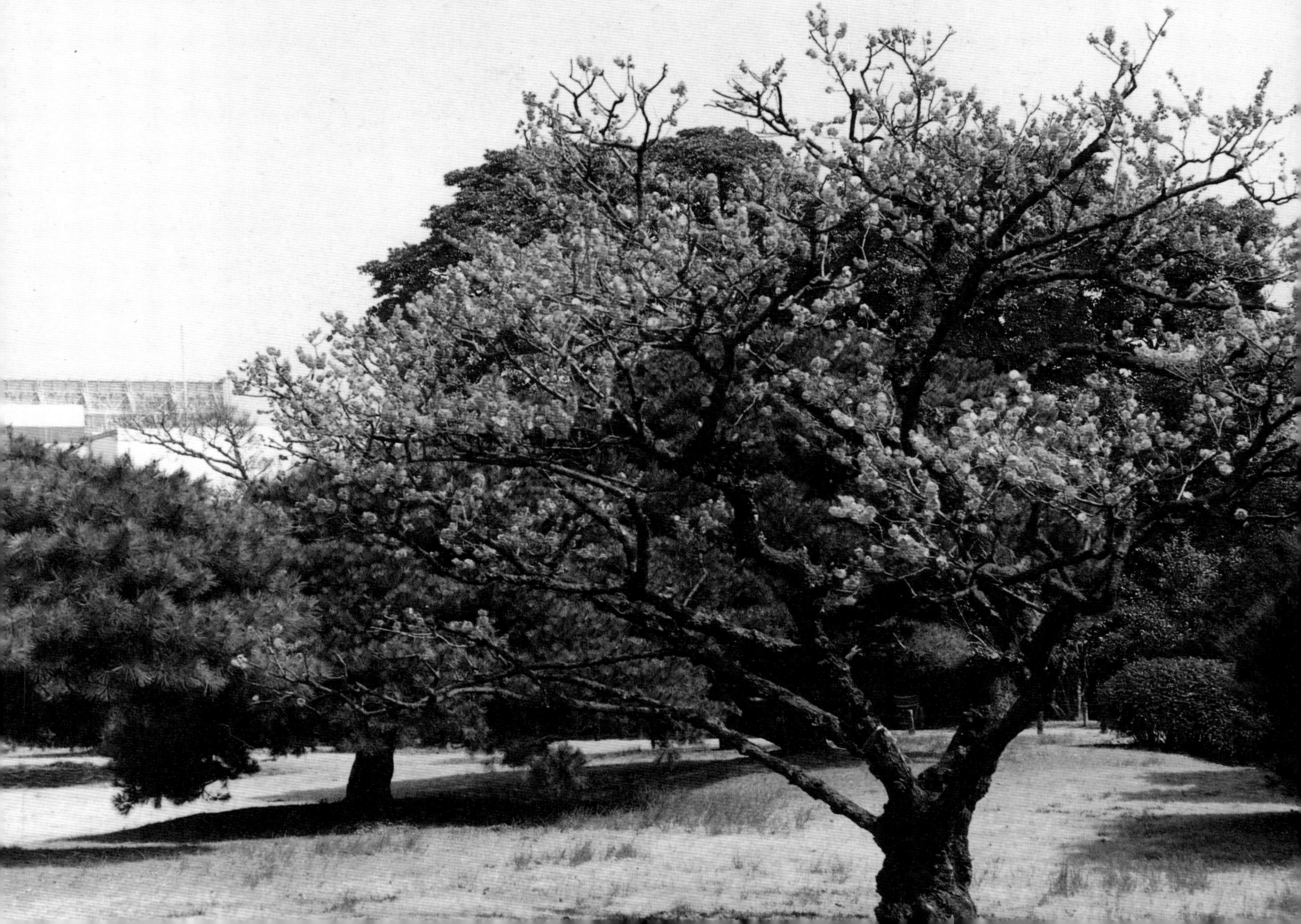

HONG KONG

SINGAPORE

ON THIS HISTORIC SITE
SIR THOMAS STAMFORD RAFFLES
FIRST LANDED IN SINGAPORE
ON 28TH JANUARY 1819
AND WITH GENIUS AND PERCEPTION
CHANGED THE DESTINY OF SINGAPORE
FROM AN OBSCURE FISHING VILLAGE
TO A GREAT SEAPORT AND
MODERN METROPOLIS

M
A
L
A
Y
S
I
A

THAILAND

DELHI & AGRA

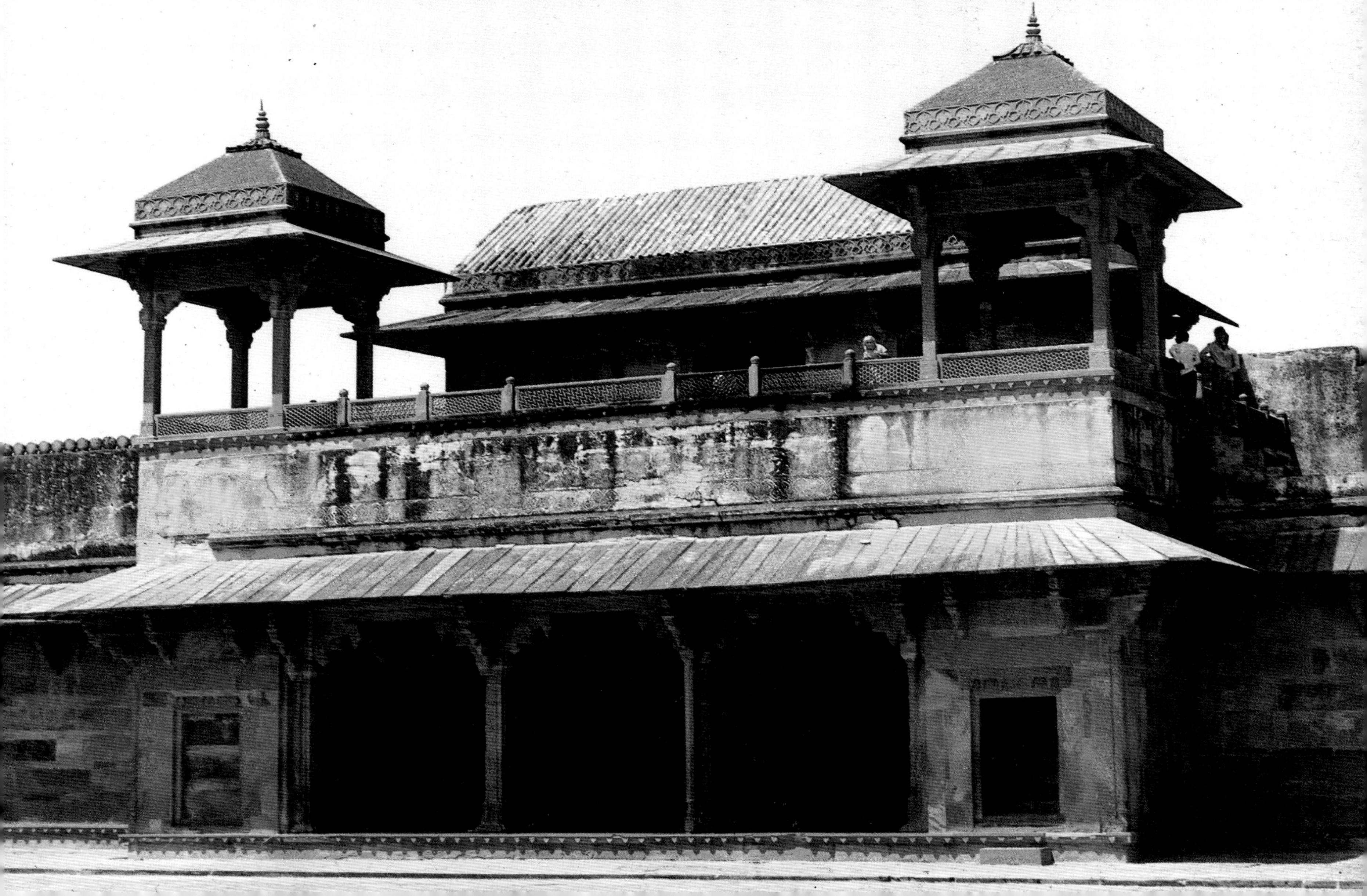

NEPAL

May Peace Prevail On Earth

DUBAI & SHARJAH

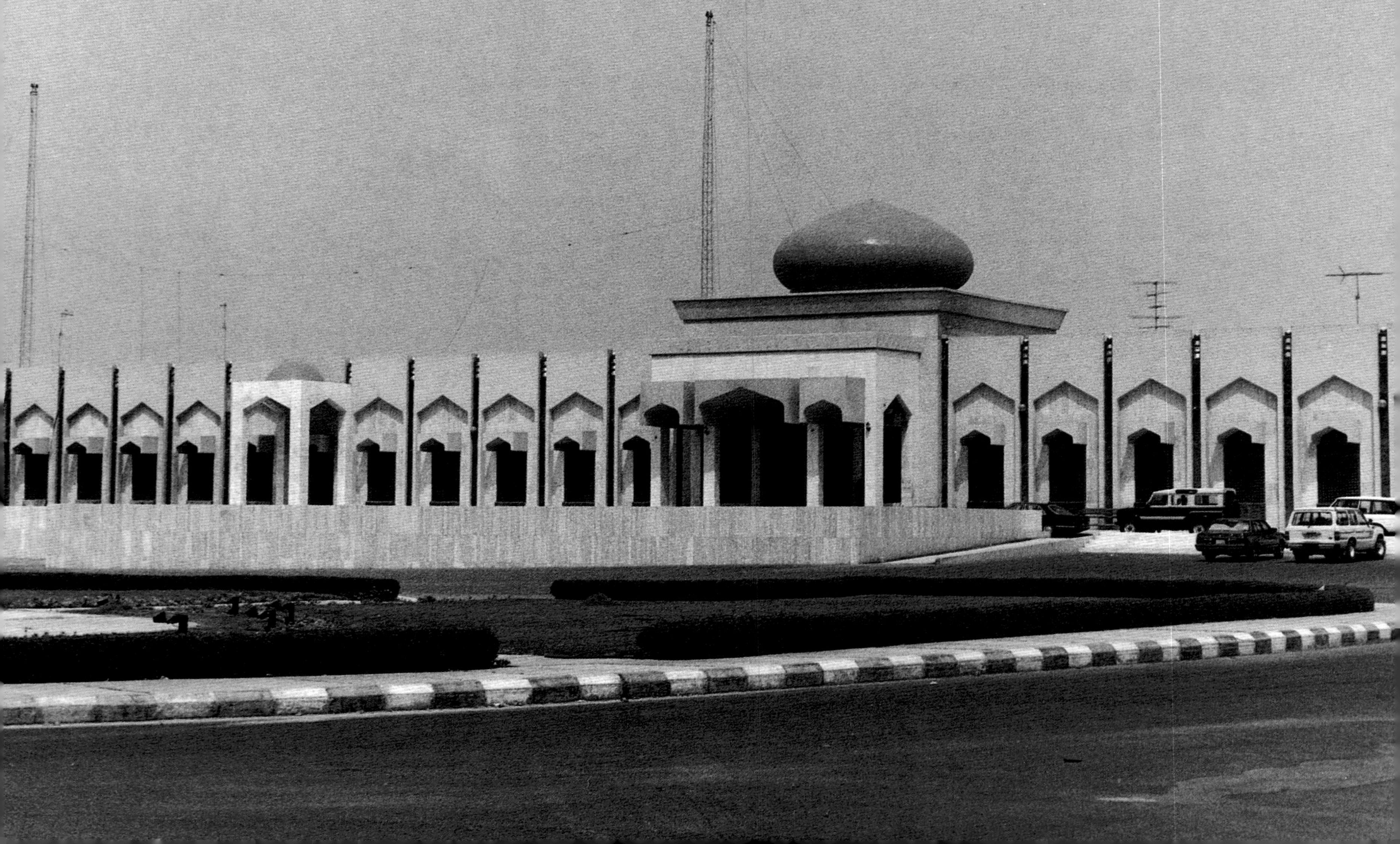

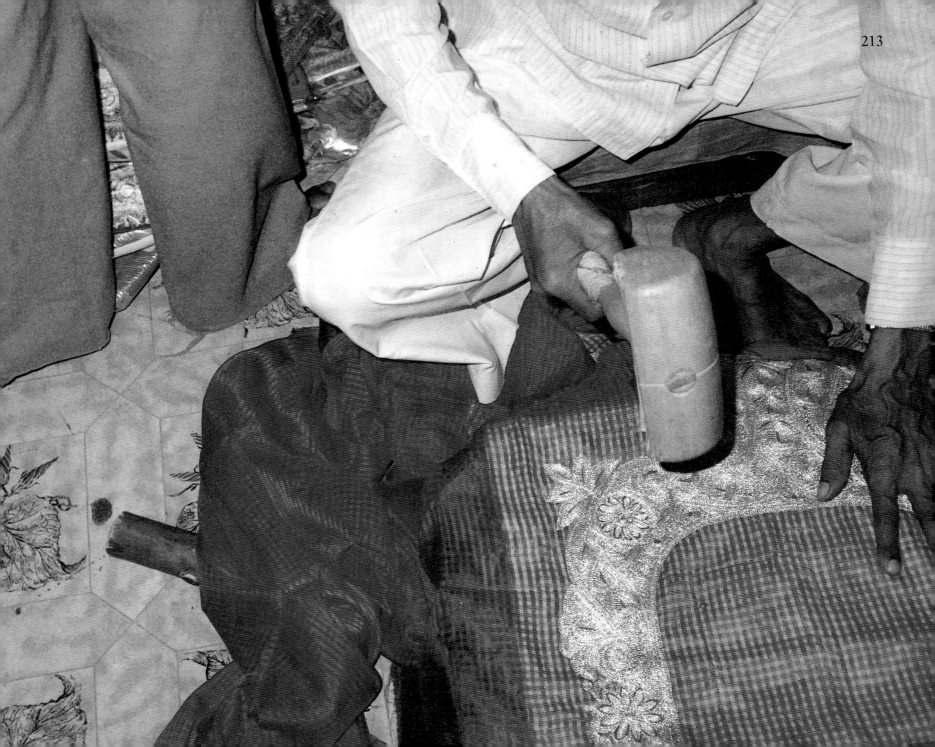

日本そして東洋　内容

まえがき

私が六歳のとき、サンタクロースは私にブラウニー・カメラを持ってきてくれました。結局これが最後のサンタクロースからのプレゼントになりました。この時期を境に、子供の世界に別れを告げ、私は冷ややかなおとなの世界へ入っていかなければなりませんでした。けれども、丁度不思議の国のアリスのように、私には逃げ込む世界、オールソープの庭がありました。その庭園で遊ぶ輝く瞳をくりくりさせるリス、私の小馬、キツネ、キジ、それにガチョウの愛らしい姿を自分の小さなカメラにおさめようと、一生懸命駆け回ったものです。アオサギが池へ向かって飛んでいき、油断している魚を急降下してさっと捕えるシーンを見たい一心で早起きし、私は茂みに腹ばいになってじっと待っていたこともあります。

日本を訪れた際、襖や七宝焼、着物などに描かれた幸運と長命の象徴である白鶴を目にして、このオールソープで子供の頃みたアオサギを思い出しました。今日では、私のカメラは人や建物に向けられることが多くなりました。この度の旅行で印象に残る数々の情景には、ひな祭りの人形の世界から抜け出して来たような可愛らしい日本の子供たち、ホンコンの中国人の商人たち、シンガポールの花嫁、アグラの象使いの少年、タイの踊り子たち、そしてネパールでは華やかな制服姿のグルカ兵の一団、行商人、山の案内人・シェルパ、聖者など、数え上げれば切りがない人々も加わっています。日本の各地で、皆様に暖かいご親切とご好意で歓迎していただきました。そして日本庭園のあの計算し尽くされたデザインに体現される、細部への心配りといったことも、決して忘れることのできない日本の思い出のひとつです。

これとは違った規模で、ニューデリーにおけるルチェンの建築物は、その比類なき壮大さとイマジネーションという点から、見逃すことのできない東洋の景観のひとつといえましょう。シンガポールでは光り輝く鮮かな緑の中、ヒマラヤを望むこの上ない静けさの丘陵と対照をなす近代的なホテル群と倉庫が連なっています。バンコックは、運河を所狭しと並ぶハウスボートあるいは高床式の小さな家々が川に向かって軒を並べ、船で通りがかりに中を見ると、そのいずれにもテレビがありました。私たちが訪れた土地は、どこでもほとんど例外なく、コンクリートが伝統的な家に取って代わり、西洋の習慣がその土地の伝統的な習慣をきかせる傾向にあるようでした。ドバイでは、この変遷をさらにもう一回転させたような情景に出会いました。整然とした街路、噴水、水泳プール、優雅な佇まいの政府庁舎などが、文字通り砂漠を征服しています。木は砂の中に根を張り、かつての荒れ地の上で草花や低木が花を咲かせています。

今回の旅は、実に忘れ難いものでした。心を奪われること、興味を覚えることの連続で、ときにおおさめようと試みたのがこのパーソナル・アルバムです。ですから国全体あるいはその国の文明を描こは悲しく、そして何度笑ったことか数え切れないほどです。こうした私の印象の数々を何とかおさうとしたものではなく、ムードや表情、建物、さり気ない一寸した場面、そしてジョークを集めることをねらいました。私が親しみを覚えた人々の暮しの一端をご一緒にご覧いただけましたらと考えております。

著者/スペンサー伯爵　1986年

不許複製

著名の文書による許可なしでの本書の複
製・転載を禁じる。

日本 および 東洋

スペンサー伯爵

日本
および
東洋